For classic scarves and fun cowls, check out this diverse collection. Most are for Beginner or Easy skill level using medium, bulky, or super bulky weight yarns.

CONTENTS

LEISURE ARTS, INC. • Maumelle, Arkansas

Garter Fringe COWL

BEGINNER

Finished Size: 8" wide (at widest area) x 20" circumference (20.5 cm x 51 cm)

Shopping List

Yarn (Medium Weight) 4

Version A

[7 ounces, 364 yards
(198 grams, 333 meters) per skein]:

- ☐ Green - 1 skein

[5 ounces, 236 yards
(141 grams, 215 meters) per skein]:

- ☐ Variegated - 1 skein

Version B

[7 ounces, 370 yards
(198 grams, 338 meters) per skein]:

- ☐ Black - 1 skein
- ☐ Maroon - 1 skein

Knitting Needles

Straight,

- ☐ Size 19 (15 mm)
  or size needed for gauge

Additional Supplies

- ☐ Crochet hook, size K (6.5 mm)
  or larger (for fringe)

Hold four strands of yarn (2 strands of **each** color) together throughout.

GAUGE INFORMATION

In Garter Stitch (knit each row),
6 sts = 4" (10 cm);
10 rows = 3" (7.5 cm)

COWL

Cast on 12 sts.

Knit each row until piece measures approximately 13" (33 cm) from cast on edge.

Next Row: (K1, P1) across.

Repeat last row for K1, P1 ribbing until piece measures approximately 20" (51 cm) from cast on edge.

Bind off all sts in **ribbing**.

FRINGE

Cut a piece of cardboard 5" (12.5 cm) wide and 12" (30.5 cm) long.
Wind the yarn **loosely** and **evenly** lengthwise around the cardboard until the card is filled, then cut across one end; repeat until you have 48 strands of yarn, 24 of **each** color.

Fold Cowl in half, matching sts of cast on and bound off edges together.

Hold two strands of **each** color yarn (4 strands total) together for each fringe; fold in half.

Using a crochet hook and inserting hook through **both** layers, draw the folded end up through a stitch and pull the loose ends through the folded end ***(Fig. A)***; draw the knot up **tightly** ***(Fig. B)***. Repeat in each st across.

Fig. A

Fig. B

Design by Marly Bird.

CLOVER

EASY

Shopping List

Yarn (Medium Weight) MEDIUM 4

[3.5 ounces, 151 yards

(100 grams, 138 meters) per skein]:

Scarf

☐ 2 skeins

Cowl

☐ 2 skeins

Knitting Needles

Straight,

☐ Size 10½ (6.5 mm)

or size needed for gauge

Additional Supplies

☐ Yarn needle (for sewing Cowl)

SIZE INFORMATION

Scarf - 4½" wide x 54" long
(11.5 cm x 137 cm)

Cowl - 10" tall x 28" circumference
(25.5 cm x 71 cm)

GAUGE INFORMATION

In pattern,
18 sts and 20 rows = 4" (10 cm)

TECHNIQUES USED

- YO *(Figs. 4a & b, page 22)*
- Slip 1 as if to **knit**, K1, PSSO *(Figs. 5a & b, page 22)*
- Slip 1 as if to **knit**, K2 tog, PSSO *(Figs. 6a & b, page 22)*
- P2 tog *(Fig. 7, page 23)*

SCARF

Cast on 21 sts.

Row 1: K3, ★ YO, slip 1 as if to **knit**, K2 tog, PSSO, YO, K3; repeat from ★ across.

Row 2: P2, P2 tog, YO, P1, YO, P2 tog, ★ P1, P2 tog, YO, P1, YO, P2 tog; repeat from ★ across to last 2 sts, P2.

Row 3: K1, K2 tog, YO, K3, ★ YO, slip 1 as if to **knit**, K2 tog, PSSO, YO, K3; repeat from ★ across to last 3 sts, YO, slip 1 as if to **knit**, K1, PSSO, K1.

Row 4: P2, YO, P2 tog, P1, P2 tog, ★ YO, P1, YO, P2 tog, P1, P2 tog; repeat from ★ across to last 2 sts, YO, P2.

Repeat Rows 1-4 for pattern until piece measures approximately 54" (137 cm) from cast on edge, ending by working Row 3.

Bind off all sts in pattern.

COWL

Cast on 45 sts.

Row 1 (Right side)**:** K3, ★ YO, slip 1 as if to **knit**, K2 tog, PSSO, YO, K3; repeat from ★ across.

Row 2: P2, P2 tog, YO, P1, YO, P2 tog, ★ P1, P2 tog, YO, P1, YO, P2 tog; repeat from ★ across to last 2 sts, P2.

Row 3: K1, K2 tog, YO, K3, ★ YO, slip 1 as if to **knit**, K2 tog, PSSO, YO, K3; repeat from ★ across to last 3 sts, YO, slip 1 as if to **knit**, K1, PSSO, K1.

Row 4: P2, YO, P2 tog, P1, P2 tog, ★ YO, P1, YO, P2 tog, P1, P2 tog; repeat from ★ across to last 2 sts, YO, P2.

Repeat Rows 1-4 for pattern until piece measures approximately 28" (71 cm) from cast on edge, ending by working Row 3.

Bind off all sts in pattern, leaving a long end for sewing.

With **right** side together, sew short ends of Cowl together.

Designs by Karen Whooley.

Knit & Rib SCARF

BEGINNER

Finished Size: Approximately 5½" wide x 54" long (14 cm x 137 cm)

Shopping List

Yarn (Medium Weight) MEDIUM 4

[6 ounces, 315 yards

(170 grams, 288 meters) per skein]:

☐ 2 skeins

Knitting Needles

Straight,

☐ Size 8 (5 mm)

or size needed for gauge

GAUGE INFORMATION

In pattern, 19 sts = 2½" (6.25 cm)

SCARF

Cast on 42 sts.

Row 1 (Right side)**:** Purl across.

Row 2: (P3, K1, P1, K1) across.

Row 3: (P3, K3) across.

Rows 4-6: Repeat Rows 2 and 3 once, then repeat Row 2 once **more**.

Row 7: Purl across.

Row 8: (K1, P1, K1, P3) across.

Row 9: (K3, P3) across.

Rows 10-12: Repeat Rows 8 and 9 once, then repeat Row 8 once **more**.

Repeat Rows 1-12 for pattern until piece measures approximately 54" (137 cm) from cast on edge, ending by working Row 6 **or** Row 12.

Bind off all sts in **knit**.

Design by Margret Willson.

Hooded SCARF

EASY

Shopping List

Yarn (Super Bulky Weight) SUPER BULKY 6

[3.5 ounces, 108 yards (100 grams, 99 meters) per skein]:

☐ 3 skeins

Knitting Needles

Straight,

☐ Size 13 (9 mm)

or size needed for gauge

Additional Supplies

☐ Yarn needle

SIZE INFORMATION

Finished Hood Width:

Small - 17½" (44.5 cm)

Medium/Large - 22½" (57 cm)

Size Note: We have printed the instructions for the sizes in different colors to make it easier for you to find:

- Small in Blue
- Medium/Large in Pink

Instructions in Black apply to both sizes.

GAUGE INFORMATION

In pattern,

12 sts (2 repeats) = 5" (12.75 cm);

15 rows = 4" (10 cm)

TECHNIQUE USED

- Adding new sts

(Figs. 3a & b, page 21)

SCARF

FIRST SIDE

Cast on 16 sts.

Rows 1 and 2: Knit across.

Row 3: P4, (K2, P4) across.

Row 4 (Right side)**:** Knit across.

Row 5: P1, K2, (P4, K2) across to last st, K1.

Row 6: Knit across.

Repeat Rows 3-6 for pattern until First Side measures approximately 20{25½}"/51{65} cm from cast on edge, ending by working Row 5.

HOOD

Row 1: Add on 6{12} sts, knit across: 22{28} sts.

Repeat Rows 3-6 of First Side until Hood measures approximately 17½{19}"/44.5{48.5} cm from added on sts, ending by working Row 5.

SECOND SIDE

Row 1: Bind off 6{12} sts, knit across: 16 sts.

Repeat Rows 3-6 of First Side until Second Side measures same as First Side, ending by working Row 5.

Last 2 Rows: Knit across.

Bind off all sts in **knit**.

Fold the Hood in half with the **right** side facing you and matching the bound off sts to the added on sts. Weave the back Hood seam across the ends of the rows from the bottom edge of the Hood to the fold as follows:

With the **right** side of both pieces facing you and edges even, sew through both sides once to secure the seam. Insert the needle under the bar **between** the first and second stitches on the row and pull the yarn through ***(Fig. A)***. Insert the needle under the next bar on the second side. Repeat from side to side, being careful to match rows.

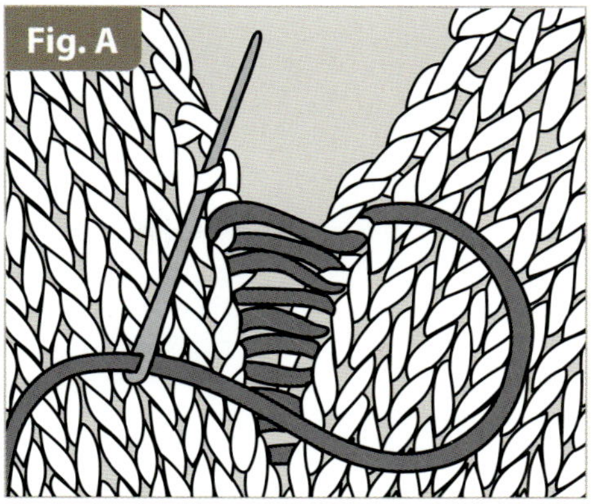

Keyhole SCARF

EASY

Finished Size: 6" wide x 30" long (15 cm x 76 cm)

Shopping List

Yarn (Bulky Weight) BULKY 5

[3.5 ounces, 120 yards

(100 grams, 109 meters) per skein]:

☐ 1 skein (either version)

Knitting Needles

Straight,

☐ Size 13 (9 mm)

or size needed for gauge

GAUGE INFORMATION

In Stockinette Stitch

(knit one row, purl one row),

12 sts and 17 rows = 4" (10 cm)

TECHNIQUE USED

• E-wrap cast on *(Fig. 1, page 21)*

STOCKINETTE STITCH VERSION

Cast on 18 sts.

Row 1: Purl across.

Row 2 (Right side)**:** Knit across.

Repeat Rows 1 and 2 for Stockinette Stitch until piece measures approximately 22" (56 cm) from cast on edge, ending by working a **purl** row.

Next Row: K7, bind off next 4 sts (keyhole), knit across: 14 sts.

Next Row: P7, e-wrap cast on 4 sts, purl across: 18 sts.

Continue in Stockinette Stitch until piece measures approximately 30" (76 cm) from cast on edge, ending by working a **purl** row.

Bind off all sts in **knit**.

GARTER STITCH EDGING VERSION

EDGING

Cast on 18 sts.

Rows 1-5: Knit across (Garter Stitch).

BODY

Row 1 (Right side)**:** Knit across.

Row 2: K3, P 12, K3.

Repeat Rows 1 and 2 for pattern until piece measures approximately 22" (56 cm) from cast on edge, ending by working a **wrong** side row.

Next Row: K7, bind off next 4 sts (keyhole), knit across: 14 sts.

Next Row: K3, P4, e-wrap cast on 4 sts, P4, K3: 18 sts.

Continue in pattern until piece measures approximately 28½" (72.5 cm) from cast on edge, ending by working a **wrong** side row.

EDGING

Rows 1-6: Knit across (Garter Stitch).

Bind off all sts in **knit**.

Design by Kim Haesemeyer.

Stockinette
Stitch Version

Garter Stitch
Edging Version

Reversible COWL

BEGINNER

Finished Size: 12½ tall x 25½" circumference (32 cm x 65 cm)

Shopping List

Yarn (Medium Weight) 4

[3 ounces, 145 yards
(85 grams 133 meters) per skein]:

☐ 2 skeins

Knitting Needles

Straight,

☐ Size 8 (5 mm) **or** size needed for gauge

Additional Supplies

☐ Yarn needle

GAUGE INFORMATION

In Stockinette Stitch
(knit one row, purl one row),
18 sts and 24 rows = 4" (10 cm)

COWL

Cast on 56 sts.

Row 1 (Right side)**:** Purl across.

Row 2: Knit across.

Row 3: P1, K5, (P2, K5) across to last st, P1.

Row 4: K1, P5, (K2, P5) across to last st, K1.

Rows 5 and 6: Repeat Rows 3 and 4.

Row 7: Purl across.

Row 8: Knit across.

Repeat Rows 3-8 for pattern until piece measures approximately 25½" (65 cm) from cast on edge, ending by working Row 6.

Bind off all sts in **knit**, leaving a long end for sewing.

With **right** side together, sew cast on and bound off edges together.

Design by Sarah J. Green.

Pom-Pom Closure COWL

INTERMEDIATE

Finished Size: 5" wide x 23" long (12.5 cm x 58.5 cm) (excluding pom-pom)

Shopping List

Yarn (Medium Weight) 4

[3.5 ounces, 151 yards (100 grams, 138 meters) per skein]:

- ☐ 4 skeins

Knitting Needles

Double pointed (set of 4),

- ☐ Size 17 (12.75 mm) **or** size needed for gauge

Additional Supplies

- ☐ Split-ring marker
- ☐ Yarn needle
- ☐ 4" (10 cm) square cardboard **or** 4" (10 cm) pom-pom maker

Hold four strands of yarn together throughout.

GAUGE INFORMATION

In Stockinette Stitch (knit each rnd), 6 sts and 8 rnds = 3" (7.5 cm)

TECHNIQUE USED

- E-wrap cast on ***(Fig. 1, page 21)***

COWL

Cast on 20 sts ***(see Using Double Pointed Needles, page 21)***. Place a split-ring marker around first st to mark the beginning of the round ***(see Markers, page 21)***.

Knit each rnd until piece measures 21" (53.5 cm) from cast on edge.

POM-POM OPENING

Rnd 1: K4, bind off next 3 sts, K 12: 17 sts.

Rnd 2: K4, e-wrap cast on 3 sts, K 13: 20 sts.

Rnds 3-5: Knit around.

Bind off all sts in **knit**.

FINISHING

Make one 4" (10 cm) pom-pom ***(Figs. 8a-c, page 23)***

Sew pom-pom to cast on edge of piece.

Use the pom-pom to connect the Cowl by pushing it through the opening.

Design by Marly Bird.

Ridged COWL

EASY

Finished Size: 17" wide by 21" circumference (43 cm x 53.5 cm)

Shopping List

Yarn (Super Bulky Weight) SUPER BULKY 6

[3.5 ounces, 108 yards

(100 grams, 99 meters) per skein]:

☐ Cream - 1 skein

☐ Grey - 1 skein

Knitting Needles

Straight,

☐ Size 15 (10 mm)

or size needed for gauge

Additional Supplies

☐ Yarn needle

GAUGE INFORMATION

In pattern,

9 sts = 4" (10 cm);

18 rows = 4¼" (10.75 cm)

COWL

With Cream, cast on 38 sts.

Row 1 (Right side)**:** Knit across.

Rows 2-4: Purl across.

Row 5: Knit across.

Rows 6 and 7: Purl across.

Row 8: Knit across.

Rows 9 and 10: Purl across.

Rows 11-13: Knit across.

Row 14: Purl across.

Rows 15 and 16: Knit across.

Row 17: Purl across.

Row 18: Knit across.

Rows 19-45: Repeat Rows 1-18 once, then repeat Rows 1-9 once **more**.

Rows 46-54: Cut Cream; with Grey, repeat Rows 10-18.

Rows 55-90: Repeat Rows 1-18 twice.

Bind off all sts in **knit**, leaving a long end for sewing.

Fold piece in half matching cast on edge to bound off edge. Using long end, weave edges together as follows:

Bring the needle from behind the work and through the center of the first stitch on the bottom piece. ★ Insert the needle behind both loops of the next stitch on the top piece ***(Fig. A)***. Insert the needle behind both loops of the inverted V of the next stitch on the bottom piece. Repeat from ★ across. Pull the yarn gently every 2 or 3 stitches, being careful to maintain even tension.

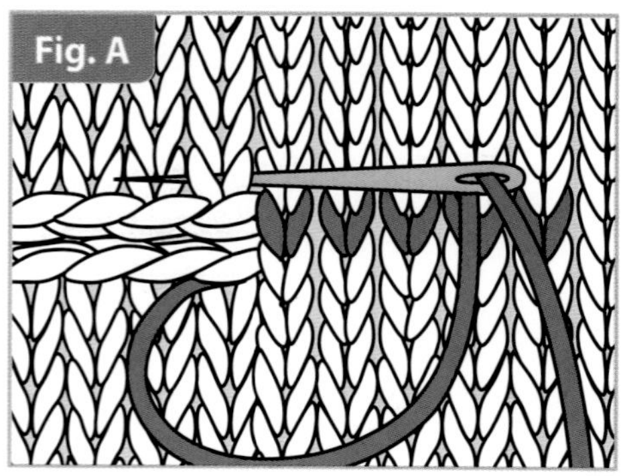

Design by Lisa Gentry.

Reversible SCARF

BEGINNER

Finished Size: Approximately 5½" wide x 51" long (14 cm x 129.5 cm)

Shopping List

Yarn (Medium Weight) MEDIUM 4

[6 ounces, 315 yards

(170 grams, 288 meters) per skein]:

☐ 2 skeins

Knitting Needles

Straight,

☐ Size 8 (5 mm) **or** size needed for gauge

GAUGE INFORMATION

In pattern, 19 sts = 2½" (6.25 cm)

SCARF

Cast on 43 sts.

Row 1: K2, (P2, K2) across to last st, P1.

Repeat Row 1 for pattern until piece measures approximately 51" (129.5 cm) from cast on edge.

Bind off all sts in **knit**.

Design by Margret Willson.

General INSTRUCTIONS

ABBREVIATIONS

cm	centimeters
K	knit
mm	millimeters
P	purl
PSSO	pass slipped stitch over
Rnd(s)	Round(s)
st(s)	stitch(es)
tog	together
YO	yarn over

Yarn Weight Symbol & Names	LACE 0	SUPER FINE 1	FINE 2	LIGHT 3	MEDIUM 4	BULKY 5	SUPER BULKY 6	JUMBO 7
Type of Yarns in Category	Fingering, size 10 crochet thread	Sock, Fingering, Baby	Sport, Baby	DK, Light Worsted	Worsted, Afghan, Aran	Chunky, Craft, Rug	Super Bulky, Roving	Jumbo, Roving
Knit Gauge Ranges in Stockinette St to 4" (10 cm)	33-40 sts**	27-32 sts	23-26 sts	21-24 sts	16-20 sts	12-15 sts	7-11 sts	6 sts and fewer
Advised Needle Size Range	000 to 1	1 to 3	3 to 5	5 to 7	7 to 9	9 to11	11 to 17	17 and larger

* GUIDELINES ONLY: The chart above reflects the most commonly used gauges and needle sizes for specific yarn categories.

** Lace weight yarns are usually knitted on larger needles to create lacy openwork patterns. Accordingly, a gauge range is difficult to determine. Always follow the gauge stated in your pattern.

SYMBOLS & TERMS

★ — work instructions following ★ as many **more** times as indicated in addition to the first time.

( ) or **[ ]** — work enclosed instructions **as many** times as specified by the number immediately following **or** contains explanatory remarks.

colon (:) — the number(s) given after a colon at the end of a row or round denote(s) the number of stitches you should have on that row or round.

BEGINNER	Projects for first-time knitters using basic knit and purl stitches. Minimal shaping.
EASY	Projects using basic stitches, repetitive stitch patterns, simple color changes, and simple shaping and finishing.
INTERMEDIATE	Projects with a variety of stitches, such as basic cables and lace, simple intarsia, double-pointed needles and knitting in the round needle techniques, mid-level shaping and finishing.
EXPERIENCED	Projects using advanced techniques and stitches, such as short rows, fair isle, more intricate intarsia, cables, lace patterns, and numerous color changes.

KNIT TERMINOLOGY		
UNITED STATES		INTERNATIONAL
gauge	=	tension
bind off	=	cast off
yarn over (YO)	=	yarn forward (yfwd) **or** yarn around needle (yrn)

KNITTING NEEDLES

U.S.	0	1	2	3	4	5	6	7	8	9	10	10½	11	13	15	17	19	35	50
U.K.	13	12	11	10	9	8	7	6	5	4	3	2	1	00	000	---	---	---	---
Metric - mm	2	2.25	2.75	3.25	3.5	3.75	4	4.5	5	5.5	6	6.5	8	9	10	12.75	15	19	25

GAUGE

Exact gauge is **essential** for proper size. Before beginning your project, make a sample swatch in the yarn and needle specified in the individual instructions. After completing the swatch, measure it, counting your stitches and rows carefully. If your swatch is larger or smaller than specified, **make another, changing needle size to get the correct gauge**. Keep trying until you find the size needles that will give you the specified gauge.

MARKERS

As a convenience to you, we have used markers to help distinguish the beginning of a round. Place a split-ring marker around first stitch in the round to indicate the beginning of the round. Move it up at the end of each round and remove it when no longer needed.

E-WRAP CAST ON

Make a backward loop with the working yarn and place it on the needle ***(Fig. 1)***.

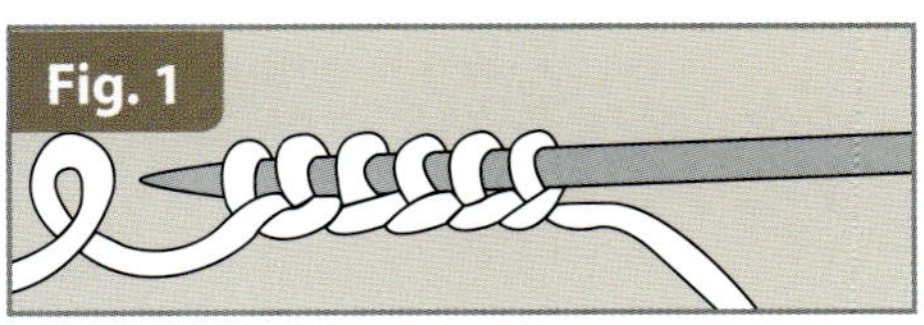

Fig. 1

USING DOUBLE POINTED NEEDLES

When working too few stitches to use a circular needle, double pointed needles are required. Divide the stitches into thirds and slip one-third of the stitches onto each of 3 double pointed needles ***(Fig. 2a)***, forming a triangle. With the fourth needle, knit across the stitches on the first needle ***(Fig. 2b)***. You will now have an empty needle with which to knit the stitches from the next needle. Work the first stitch of each needle firmly to prevent gaps.

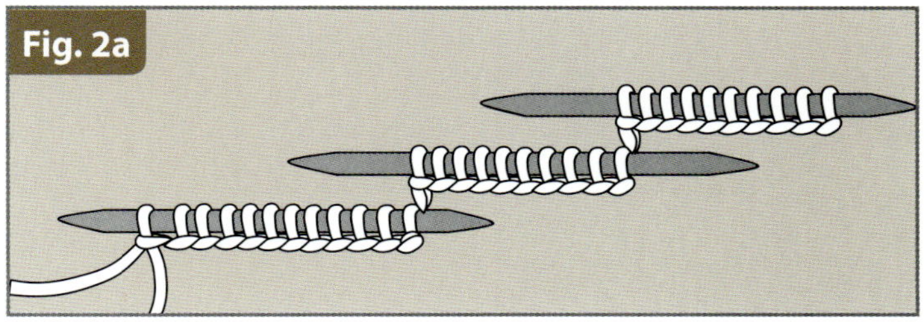

Fig. 2a

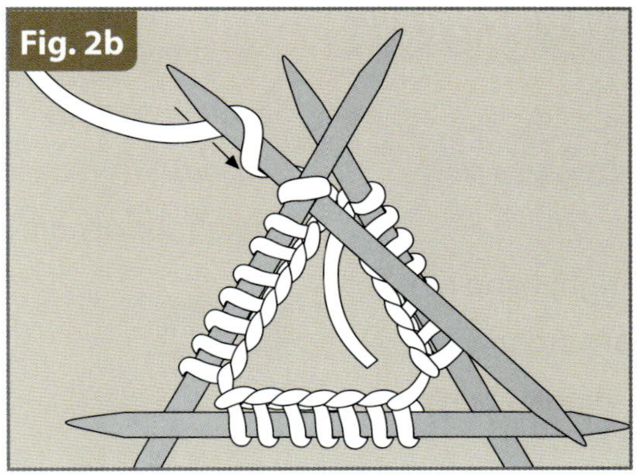

Fig. 2b

INCREASES

ADDING NEW STITCHES

Insert the right needle into stitch as if to **knit**, yarn over and pull loop through ***(Fig. 3a)***, insert the left needle into the loop just worked from **front** to **back** and slip the loop onto the left needle ***(Fig. 3b)***. Repeat for required number of stitches.

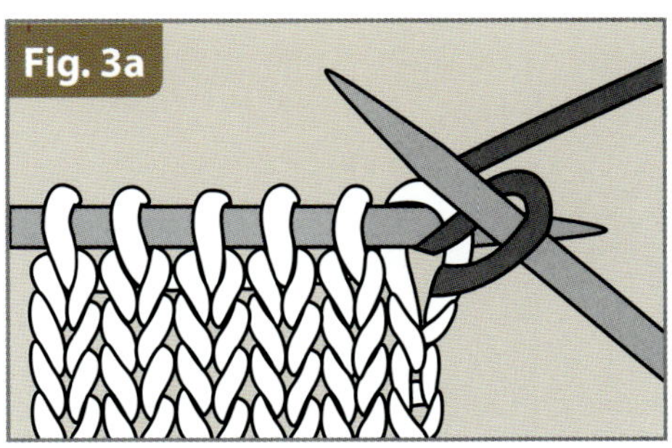

Fig. 3a

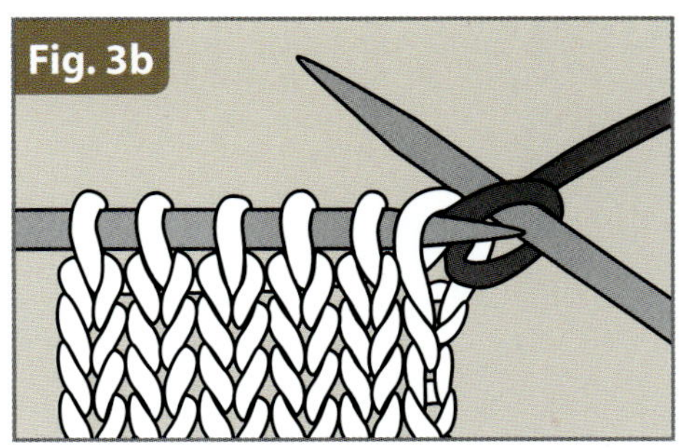

Fig. 3b

YARN OVER *(abbreviated YO)*

After a knit stitch, before a knit stitch

Bring the yarn forward **between** the needles, then back **over** the top of the right hand needle, so that it is now in position to knit the next stitch *(Fig. 4a)*.

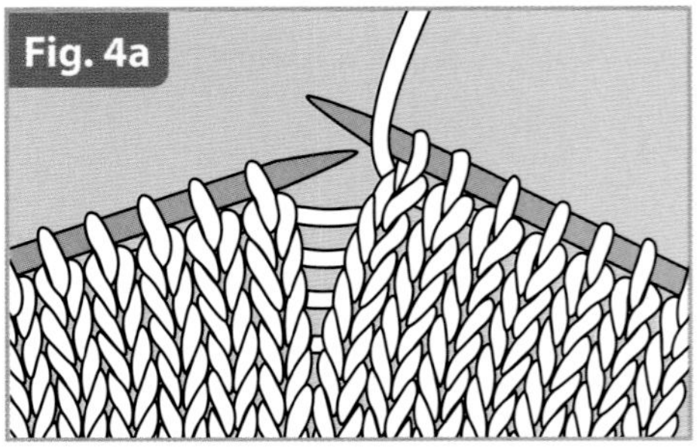

Fig. 4a

After a purl stitch, before a purl stitch

Take yarn **over** the right hand needle to the back, then forward **under** it, so that it is now in position to purl the next stitch *(Fig. 4b)*.

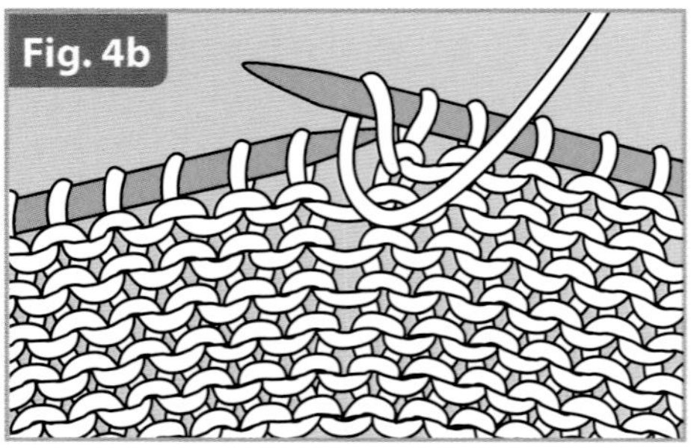

Fig. 4b

DECREASES

SLIP 1, KNIT 1, PASS SLIPPED STITCH OVER

(abbreviated slip 1, K1, PSSO)

Slip one stitch as if to **knit** ***(Fig. 5a)***. Knit the next stitch. With the left needle, bring the slipped stitch over the knit stitch ***(Fig. 5b)*** and off the needle.

Fig. 5a

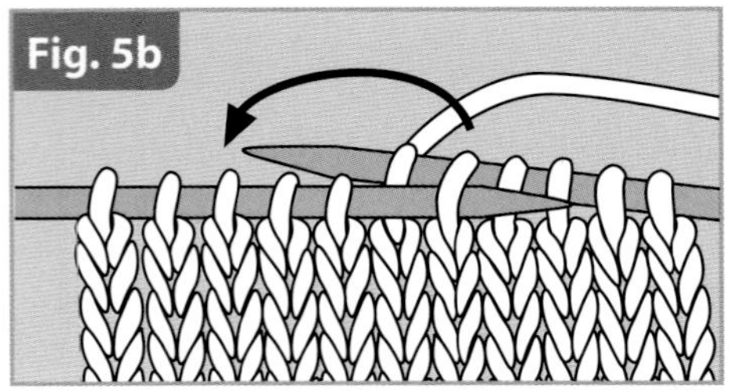

Fig. 5b

SLIP 1, KNIT 2 TOGETHER, PASS SLIPPED STITCH OVER

(abbreviated slip 1, K2 tog, PSSO)

Slip one stitch as if to **knit** ***(Fig. 5a)***, then knit the next two stitches together ***(Fig. 6a)***. With the left needle, bring the slipped stitch over the stitch just made and off the needle ***(Fig. 6b)***.

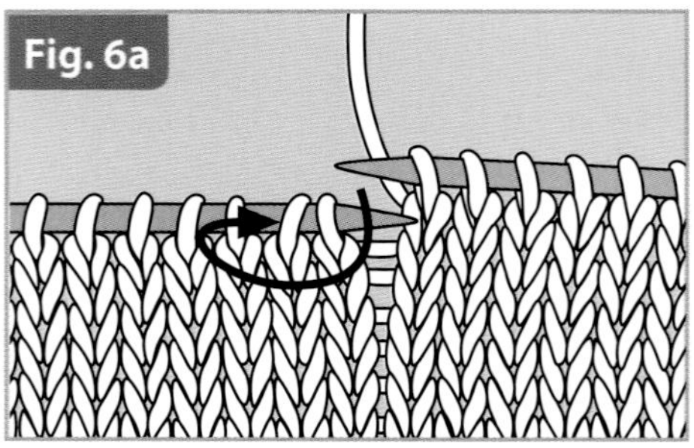

Fig. 6a

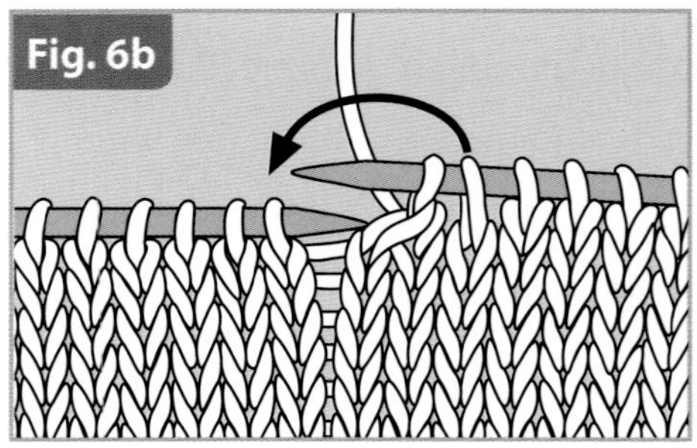

Fig. 6b

PURL 2 TOGETHER

(abbreviated P2 tog)

Insert the right needle into the **front** of the first two stitches on the left needle as if to **purl** ***(Fig. 7)***, then **purl** them together as if they were one stitch.

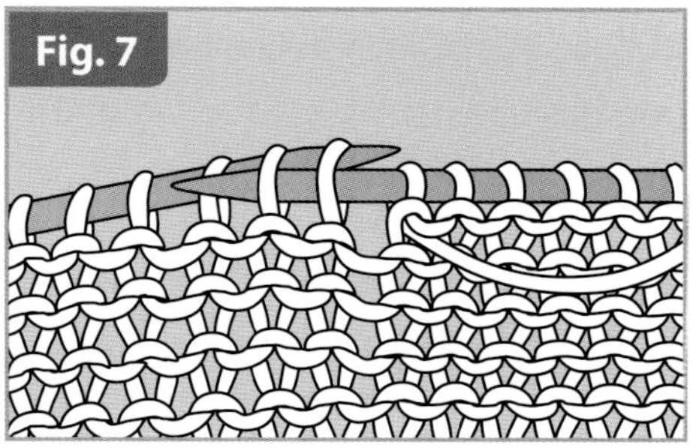
Fig. 7

POM-POM

Wind the yarn around the cardboard until it is approximately ½" (12 mm) thick in the middle ***(Fig. 8a)***. Carefully slip the yarn off the cardboard and firmly tie an 18" (45.5 cm) length of yarn around the middle ***(Fig. 8b)***. Leave yarn ends long enough to attach the pom-pom. Cut the loops on both ends and trim the pom-pom into a smooth ball ***(Fig. 8c)***.

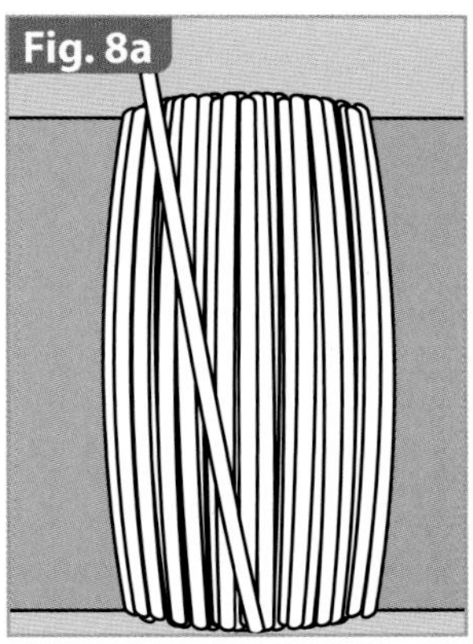
Fig. 8a

Fig. 8b

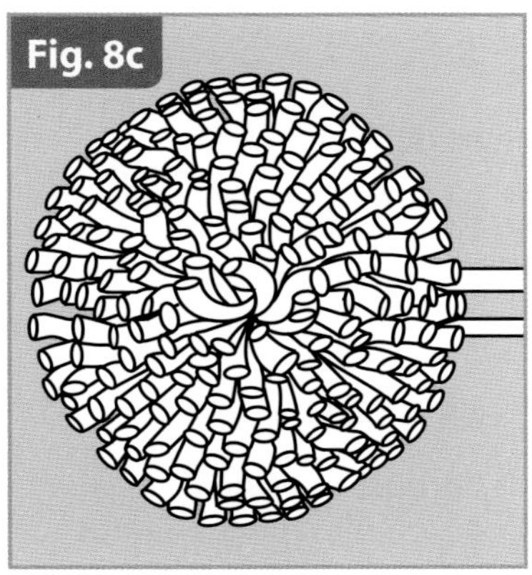
Fig. 8c

Yarn INFORMATION

Items in this book were made using various weights of yarn. Any brand of the specified weight of yarn may be used. It is best to refer to the yardage/meters when determining how many balls or skeins to purchase. Remember, to arrive at the finished size, it is the GAUGE/TENSION that is important, not the brand of yarn.

For your convenience, listed below are the specific yarns used to create our photography models. Because yarn manufacturers make frequent changes in their product lines, you may sometimes find it necessary to use a substitute yarn or to search for the discontinued product at alternate suppliers (locally or online).

GARTER FRINGE COWL

Version A

Red Heart® Super Saver®

Green - #0672 Spring Green

Variegated - #0964 Primary

Version B

Red Heart® With Love®

Black - #1012 Black

Maroon - #1907 Boysenberry

CLOVER SCARF

Red Heart® Treasure™

#1923 Tapestry

CLOVER COWL

Red Heart® Treasure™

#1918 Abstract

KNIT & RIB SCARF

Caron® Simply Soft®

#9765 Pumpkin

HOODED SCARF

Bernat® Softee® Chunky™

#28342 Teal Twists

KEYHOLE SCARF

Bernat® Roving™

#00011 Bark

REVERSIBLE COWL

Lion Brand® Vanna's Choice®

#302 Taupe Mist

POM-POM CLOSURE COWL

Red Heart® Treasure™

#1919 Watercolors

RIDGED COWL

Bernat® Softee® Chunky™

Cream - #28008 Natural

Grey - #28041 Clay

REVERSIBLE SCARF

Caron® Simply Soft®

#9783 Taupe

We have made every effort to ensure that these instructions are accurate and complete. We cannot, however, be responsible for human error, typographical mistakes, or variations in individual work.

Production Team: Instructional/Technical Editor - Sarah J. Green; Editorial Writer - Susan Frantz Wiles; Senior Graphic Artist - Lora Puls; and Graphic Artist - Leia Morshedi.

Copyright © 2017 by Leisure Arts, Inc., 104 Champs Blvd., STE 100, Maumelle, AR 72113, www.leisurearts.com. All rights reserved. This publication is protected under federal copyright laws. Reproduction or distribution of this publication or any other Leisure Arts publication, including publications which are out of print, is prohibited unless specifically authorized. This includes, but is not limited to, any form of reproduction or distribution on or through the Internet, including posting, scanning, or e-mail transmission.